Basic Christianity

JOHN STOTT

with Dale & Sandy Larsen

**6 studies
for individuals or groups**

CHRISTIAN BASICS BIBLE STUDIES

With Guidelines for
Leaders & Study Notes
NIV Text Included

INTERVARSITY PRESS
DOWNERS GROVE, ILLINOIS, USA
LEICESTER, ENGLAND

InterVarsity Press
P.O. Box 1400, Downers Grove, IL 60515, USA
38 De Montfort Street, Leicester LE1 7GP, England

InterVarsity Press®, U.S.A., is the book-publishing division of InterVarsity Christian Fellowship®, a student movement active on campus at hundreds of universities, colleges and schools of nursing in the United States of America, and a member movement of the International Fellowship of Evangelical Students. For information about local and regional activities, write Public Relations Dept., InterVarsity Christian Fellowship, 6400 Schroeder Rd., P.O. Box 7895, Madison, WI 53707-7895.

Inter-Varsity Press, England, is the book-publishing division of the Universities and Colleges Christian Fellowship (formerly the Inter-Varsity Fellowship), a student movement linking Christian Unions in universities and colleges throughout the United Kingdom and the Republic of Ireland, and a member movement of the International Fellowship of Evngelical Students. For information about local and national activities write to UCCF, 38 De Montfort Street, Leicester LE1 7GP.

This study guide is based on and adapts material from Basic Christianity by John R. W. Stott ©1958, 1971 by Inter-Varsity Press. Some notes in Study 3 are taken from "The Upper Room Discourse" by John R. W. Stott in Christ the Liberator ©1971 by Inter-Varsity Christian Fellowship of the United States of America.

Cover photograph: Michael Goss
Cover background: Cowgirl Stock Photography ©1991

USA ISBN 0-8308-2002-7
UK ISBN 0-85111-340-0

Printed in the United States of America ♾

15   14   13   12   11   10   9   8   7   6   5   4   3   2   1

04   03   02   01   00   99   98   97   96   95   94

Getting the Most Out of Christian Basics Bible Studies

The essentials of our faith: knowing Christ, understanding Scripture, following Jesus in all areas of life, learning how to pray in the midst of a busy life, understanding how our faith is lived out at work, experiencing true worship, developing Christian character, and setting priorities that are godly. These are the topics in this series designed to help you become a more mature believer.

What Kind of Guide Is This?
The studies are not designed to merely tell you what one person thinks. Instead, through inductive study, they will help you discover for yourself what Scripture is saying. Each study deals with a particular passage—rather than jumping around the Bible—so that you can really delve into the author's meaning in that context.

The studies ask three different kinds of questions. *Observation* questions help you to understand the content of the passage by asking about the basic facts: who, what, when, where and how. *Interpretation* questions delve into the meaning of the passage. *Application* questions help you discover its implications for growing in Christ. These three keys unlock the treasures of the biblical writings and help you live them out.

This is a thought-provoking guide. Each question assumes a variety of answers. Many questions do not have "right" answers, particularly questions that aim at meaning or application. Instead, the questions should inspire users to explore the passage more thoroughly.

This study guide is flexible. You can use it for individual study, but it is also great for a variety of groups—student, professional, neighborhood or church groups. Each study takes about forty-five minutes in a group setting or thirty minutes in personal study.

How They're Put Together
Each study is composed of four sections: opening paragraphs and questions to help you get into the topic, the NIV text and questions that invite study of the passage, questions to help you apply what you have learned, and a suggestion for prayer.

The workbook format provides space for writing a response to each question. This format is ideal for personal study and allows group members to prepare in advance for the discussion and/or write down notes during the study. This space can form a permanent record of your thoughts and spiritual progress.

At the back of the guide are study notes which may be useful for leaders or for individuals. These notes do not give "the answers," but they do provide additional background information on certain questions to help you through the difficult spots.

The "Guidelines for Leaders" section describes how to lead a group discussion, gives helpful tips on group dynamics and suggests ways to deal with problems which may arise during the discussion. With such helps, someone with little or no experience can lead an effective group study.

Suggestions for Individual Study

1. If you have not read the book or booklet suggested in the "further reading" section, you may want to read the portion suggested before you begin your study.

2. Read the introduction. Consider the opening questions and note your responses.

3. Pray, asking God to speak to you from his Word about this particular topic.

4. Read the passage reproduced for you in the New International Version. You may wish to mark phrases that seem important. Note in the margin any questions that come to your mind as you read.

5. Use the questions from the study guide to more thoroughly examine the passage. Note your findings in the space provided. After you have made your own notes, read the corresponding study notes in the back of the book for further insights.

6. Reread the entire passage, making further notes about its general principles and about the way you intend to use them.

7. Move to the "commit" section. Spend time prayerfully considering what the passage has to say specifically to your life.

8. Read the suggestion for prayer. Speak to God about insights you have gained. Tell him of any desires you have for specific growth. Ask him to help you as you attempt to live out the principles described in that passage.

Suggestions for Members of a Group Study

Joining a Bible study group can be a great avenue to spiritual growth. Here are a few guidelines that will help you as you participate in the studies in this guide.

1. These studies focus on a particular passage of Scripture—in depth. Only rarely should you refer to other portions of the Bible, and then only at the request of the leader. Of course, the Bible is internally consistent. Other good forms of study draw on that consistency, but inductive Bible study sticks with a single passage and works on it in depth.

2. These are discussion studies. Questions in this guide aim at helping a group discuss together a passage of Scripture in order to understand its content, meaning and implications. Most people are either natural talkers or natural listeners. Yet this type of study works best if people participate more or less evenly. Try to curb any natural tendency to either excessive talking or excessive quiet. You and the rest of the group will benefit.

3. Most questions in this guide allow for a variety of answers. If you disagree with someone else's comment, gently say so. Then explain your own point of view from the passage before you.

4. Be willing to lead a discussion, if asked. Much of the preparation for leading has already been accomplished in the writing of this guide.

5. Respect the privacy of people in your group. Many people speak of things within the context of a Bible study/prayer group that they do not want to be public knowledge. Assume that personal information spoken within the group setting is private, unless you are specifically told otherwise. And don't talk about it elsewhere.

6. We recommend that all groups follow a few basic guidelines and that these guidelines be read at the first session. The guidelines, which you may wish to adapt to your situation, are the following:

a. Anything said in this group is considered confidential and will not be discussed outside the group unless specific permission is given to do so.

b. We will provide time for each person present to talk if he or she feels comfortable doing so.

c. We will talk about ourselves and our own situations, avoiding conversation about other people.

d. We will listen attentively to each other.

e. We will pray for each other.

7. Enjoy your study. Prepare to grow. God bless.

Suggestions for Group Leaders

There are specific suggestions to help you in leading in the guidelines for leaders and in the study notes at the back of this guide. Read the guidelines for leaders carefully, even if you are only leading one group meeting. Then you can go to the section on the particular session you will lead.

Introduction: God Is Seeking Us

Many people visualize a God who sits comfortably on a distant throne, remote, aloof, uninterested and indifferent to the needs of mortals, until, it may be, they can badger him into taking action on their behalf. Such a view is wholly false.

The Bible reveals a God who, long before it even occurs to us to turn to him, while we are still lost in darkness and sunk in sin, takes the initiative, rises from his throne, lays aside his glory and stoops to seek until we find him.

God has created. God has spoken. God has acted. These statements of God's initiative summarize the message of the whole of Scripture. This study guide deals with the second and third actions of God, because basic Christianity begins with the historical figure of Jesus Christ. If God has acted, his noblest act is the redemption of the world through Jesus Christ.

God has spoken and acted in Jesus Christ. He has said something. He has done something. This means that Christianity is not just pious talk. It is neither a collection of religious ideas nor a catalog of rules. It is not primarily an invitation to us to do anything; it is supremely a declaration of what God has done in Christ for human beings like ourselves.

Come, and discover the Christ who seeks you. You may meet Christ for the first time, or you may meet him again in a fresh and deeper way.

For further reading: Preface of Basic Christianity.

Study One
Are You Ready to Meet Christ?

Mark 10:17-31

I remember a young man coming to see me when he had just left school and begun work in London. He had given up going to church, he said, because he could not say the Creed without being a hypocrite. He no longer believed it. When he had finished his explanations, I said to him, "If I were to answer your problems to your complete intellectual satisfaction, would you be willing to alter your manner of life?" He smiled slightly and blushed. His real problem was not intellectual but moral.

This, then, is the spirit in which our search must be conducted. We must cast aside apathy, pride, prejudice and sin, and seek God in scorn of the consequences.

Open

☐ What are two or three of your biggest questions about Jesus Christ?

☐ When you think of total commitment to Christ, what is most unsettling about the idea?

__He might want me to do something I don't want to do.

__I have too many other issues to deal with right now.

__He might want me to give up something I want to keep.

__What if he's not real?

__He might let me down.

__I don't want to be ridiculed for my beliefs.

__other:_____

Study

Read Mark 10:17-31:

[17] As Jesus started on his way, a man ran up to him and fell on his knees before him. "Good teacher," he asked, "what must I do to inherit eternal life?"

[18] "Why do you call me good?" Jesus answered. "No one is good—except God alone. [19] You know the commandments: 'Do not murder, do not commit adultery, do not steal, do not give false testimony, do not defraud, honor your father and mother.' "

[20] "Teacher," he declared, "all these I have kept since I was a boy."

[21] Jesus looked at him and loved him. "One thing you lack," he said. "Go, sell everything you have and give to the poor, and you will have treasure in heaven. Then come, follow me."

[22] At this the man's face fell. He went away sad, because he had great wealth.

[23] Jesus looked around and said to his disciples, "How hard it is for the rich to enter the kingdom of God!"

[24] The disciples were amazed at his words. But Jesus said again, "Children, how hard it is to enter the kingdom of God! [25] It is easier for a camel to go through the eye of a needle than for a rich man to enter the kingdom of God."

[26] The disciples were even more amazed, and said to each other, "Who then can be saved?"

[27] Jesus looked at them and said, "With man this is impossible, but not with God; all things are possible with God."

[28] Peter said to him, "We have left everything to follow you!"

[29] "I tell you the truth," Jesus replied, "no one who has left home or brothers or sisters or mother or father or children or fields for me and the gospel [30] will fail to receive a hundred times as much in this present age (homes, brothers, sisters, mothers, children and fields—and with them, persecutions) and in the age to come, eternal life. [31] But many who are first will be last, and the last first."

1. What admirable qualities did the wealthy man display?

2. How did Jesus reveal the area of unwillingness in the man's heart?

3. When Jesus told the man to sell everything and give away the proceeds, the man responded immediately—by getting up off his knees and walking away. What do you think he had decided which made him do that?

4. Fear is the greatest enemy of truth and can paralyze anyone who searches for truth. How do you see fear—or apathy, pride, prejudice and sin—working in the rich man's life?

5. Where do you see those hindrances in your own life?

6. Jesus looked at the man and "loved him." What encouragement do you draw from Jesus' attitude toward this seeker?

7. Christ is very open about the cost of following him. What benefits does he promise for those willing to pay that cost?

Commit ——————————————————————————

☐ The rich man asked Jesus a theological question but was not satisfied with the answer. How willing are you to hear and obey the answers Jesus gives to your questions about him?

☐ Jesus went right to the point of the wealthy man's greatest obstacle to faith: he asked the man to give away his wealth. If you were that man, what do you think Jesus would ask you to do?

Open your mind and heart to God in Jesus Christ. Tell him that you are ready to be confronted by him no matter how unsettling or inconvenient it is.

For further reading: Chapter one of Basic Christianity.

Study Two
The Claims of Christ

John 8:51-59

Jesus claimed an intimate relationship to God—Son to Father. That Jesus claimed this is confirmed by the indignation which he aroused in the Jews. He "made himself the Son of God," they said. So close was his identification with God that it was natural for him to equate a person's attitude to himself with that person's attitude to God. Thus,

to know him was to know God;

to see him was to see God;

to believe in him was to believe in God;

to receive him was to receive God;

to hate him was to hate God;

to honor him was to honor God.

Open

☐ How do your mental images of God and Jesus differ?

☐ How are those images similar (or identical)?

☐ To what extent do you associate your attitude toward Jesus with your attitude toward God?

Study

Read John 8:51-59:

[51] [In controversy with Jewish religious leaders, Jesus said,] "I tell you the truth, if anyone keeps my word, he will never see death."

[52] At this the Jews exclaimed, "Now we know that you are demon-possessed! Abraham died and so did the prophets, yet you say that if anyone keeps your word, he will never taste death. [53] Are you greater than our father Abraham? He died, and so did the prophets. Who do you think you are?"

[54] Jesus replied, "If I glorify myself, my glory means nothing. My Father, whom you claim as your God, is the one who glorifies me. [55] Though you do not know him, I know him. If I said I did

not, I would be a liar like you, but I do know him and keep his word. [56] Your father Abraham rejoiced at the thought of seeing my day; he saw it and was glad."

[57] "You are not yet fifty years old," the Jews said to him, "and you have seen Abraham!"

[58] "I tell you the truth," Jesus answered, "before Abraham was born, I am!" [59] At this, they picked up stones to stone him, but Jesus hid himself, slipping away from the temple grounds.

---

1. Jesus had a unique claim to special intimacy with God. What examples of his claim do you find in this passage?

---

2. Why do you think Jesus could say, "If anyone keeps my word, he will never see death"?

---

3. How does this claim about power over death show Jesus' understanding of his own equality with God?

---

4. To claim that he existed before Abraham, Jesus could have said, "Before Abraham was born, I was." Instead he said, "I am." To understand the impact of those words on the Jewish religious leaders, look at how God answered Moses' question about God's name: "God said to Moses, 'I AM WHO I AM. This is what you are to say to the Israelites: "I AM has sent me to you" ' " (Exodus 3:14). In that light, what does Jesus' use of the present tense say about who he claimed to be?

5. Imagine yourself today hearing a person say the things Jesus said in this passage. What conclusions could you draw about that person? (Think of several alternate conclusions.)

6. What further evidence would you look for in order to evaluate the person's claims?

7. If everything Jesus said here is true, what difference does it make—to the world at large?

to you personally?

Commit

☐ If you are not sure you believe what Jesus said about himself, commit yourself to further investigation.

☐ If what you have read today has raised some new ideas, trust God to clarify what he wants you to know.

Ask God to show you what to think of Jesus Christ.

For further reading: Chapter two of Basic Christianity.

Study Three
The Character of Christ

John 13:1-17

Some years ago I received a letter from a young man I knew slightly. "I have just made a great discovery," he wrote. "Almighty God had two sons. Jesus Christ was the first; I am the second." I glanced at the address at the top of the letter. He was writing from a well-known mental hospital.

There have of course been many pretenders to greatness and to divinity. Lunatic asylums are full of deluded people who claim to be Julius Caesar, the Prime Minister, the Emperor of Japan or Jesus Christ. But no one believes them. No one is deceived except themselves. They have no disciples, except perhaps other patients. They fail to convince other people simply because they do not seem to be what they claim to be. Their character does not support their claims.

The Christian's conviction about Christ is greatly strengthened by the fact that he does appear to be who he said he was. There is no discrepancy between his words and his deeds.

Open

☐ When have you been deceived by someone who turned out not to be what he or she seemed?

☐ How did you find out the truth?

Study

Read John 13:1-17:

[1]It was just before the Passover Feast. Jesus knew that the time had come for him to leave this world and go to the Father. Having loved his own who were in the world, he now showed them the full extent of his love.

[2]The evening meal was being served, and the devil had already prompted Judas Iscariot, son of Simon, to betray Jesus. [3]Jesus knew that the Father had put all things under his power, and that he had come from God and was returning to God; [4]so he got up from the meal, took off his outer clothing, and wrapped a towel around his waist. [5]After that, he poured water into a basin and began to wash his disciples' feet, drying them with the towel that was wrapped around him.

[6]He came to Simon Peter, who said to him, "Lord, are you going to wash my feet?"

[7]Jesus replied, "You do not realize now what I am doing, but later you will understand."

[8]"No," said Peter, "you shall never wash my feet."

Jesus answered, "Unless I wash you, you have no part with me."

[9]"Then, Lord," Simon Peter replied, "not just my feet but my hands and my head as well!"

[10] Jesus answered, "A person who has had a bath needs only to wash his feet; his whole body is clean. And you are clean, though not every one of you." [11]For he knew who was going to betray him, and that was why he said not every one was clean.

[12] When he had finished washing their feet, he put on his clothes and returned to his place. "Do you understand what I have done for you?" he asked them. [13]"You call me 'Teacher' and 'Lord,' and rightly so, for that is what I am. [14]Now that I, your Lord and Teacher, have washed your feet, you also should wash one another's feet. [15] I have set you an example that you should do as I have done for you. [16] I tell you the truth, no servant is greater than his master, nor is a messenger greater than the one who sent him. [17] Now that you know these things, you will be blessed if you do them."

---

1. Jesus "knew that the Father had put all things under his power, and that he had come from God and was returning to God." What did he do as a result of this knowledge (vv. 3-4)?

---

2. How does his action contradict what we would expect a person with such knowledge to do?

---

3. Why do you think Peter protested at having his feet washed by Jesus?

4. Jesus exhibited both the greatest self-esteem and the greatest self-sacrifice. How are both qualities demonstrated in his menial work of washing his disciples' feet?

5. Jesus acknowledged himself as "Teacher" and "Lord" while setting the example of footwashing (vv. 13-15). How would you describe the character of that sort of Lord and Teacher?

6. Put yourself in Peter's sandals. How would you have reacted when Jesus started to wash your feet?

Commit

☐ How will your life be affected if you have a Lord and Teacher with the character of Jesus?

☐ In order to have Jesus as your Lord and Teacher, how must he "wash" you?

Search your heart to be sure you are willing, then ask Jesus to be your Teacher and Lord.

For further reading: Chapter three of Basic Christianity.

Study Four
The Resurrection of Christ

Luke 24:36-48

O f the resurrection Luke, who is known to have been a painstaking and accurate historian, says there are "many proofs." We may not feel able to go so far as Thomas Arnold, who called the resurrection "the best attested fact in history," but certainly many impartial students have judged the evidence to be extremely good. For instance, Sir Edward Clarke K.C. wrote to the Reverend E. L. Macassey:

As a lawyer I have made a prolonged study of the evidences for the events of the first Easter Day. To me the evidence is conclusive, and over and over again in the High Court I have secured the verdict on evidence not nearly so compelling. Inference follows on evidence, and a truthful witness is always artless and disdains effect. The Gospel evidence for the resurrection is of this class, and as a lawyer I accept it unreservedly as the testimony of truthful men to facts they were able to substantiate.

Open

☐ How do you go about proving or disproving something?

__I talk to people I trust.

__I don't think we can prove
anything for sure.

__If something feels right,
I tend to believe it, and if
it doesn't feel right, I
don't believe it.

__As far as I'm concerned,
seeing is believing.

__I gather the facts and draw
my own conclusions.

__other:_____

☐ How do you respond to the idea that someone could come back from the dead by his own decision and under his own power?

Study

On the Sunday after he was crucified, Jesus appeared to two people on the road from Jerusalem to Emmaus. They rushed to the eleven remaining disciples and reported to them. Read Luke 24:36-48:

³⁶ While they were still talking about this, Jesus himself stood among them and said to them, "Peace be with you."

³⁷ They were startled and frightened, thinking they saw a ghost. ³⁸ He said to them, "Why are you troubled, and why do doubts rise in your minds? ³⁹ Look at my hands and my feet. It is I myself! Touch me and see; a ghost does not have flesh and bones, as you see I have."

⁴⁰ When he had said this, he showed them his hands and feet.

⁴¹And while they still did not believe it because of joy and amazement, he asked them, "Do you have anything here to eat?" ⁴²They gave him a piece of broiled fish, ⁴³and he took it and ate it in their presence.

⁴⁴He said to them, "This is what I told you while I was still with you: Everything must be fulfilled that is written about me in the Law of Moses, the Prophets and the Psalms."

⁴⁵Then he opened their minds so they could understand the Scriptures. ⁴⁶He told them, "This is what is written: The Christ will suffer and rise from the dead on the third day, ⁴⁷and repentance and forgiveness of sins will be preached in his name to all nations, beginning at Jerusalem. ⁴⁸You are witnesses of these things."

---

1. Why would the disciples be frightened at the prospect of the ghost of Jesus, but joyful at the prospect of Jesus in the flesh?

---

2. What proof did Jesus offer that he was not only spiritually alive but physically alive?

---

3. In order to investigate for themselves whether he had a physical body, what did Jesus invite the disciples to do?

4. How does Jesus' resurrection confirm what the Old Testament Scriptures predicted about him?

5. We do not have Jesus present with us in the flesh; we can't touch him or watch him eat. What evidence do you have for his rising from the dead and being alive today?

6. What is your conclusion from examining the evidence of Jesus' resurrection?

Commit ────────────────────────────

☐ How is your life different because Jesus is alive?

☐ What further changes would you like to see in your life because Jesus lives?

☐ If you still doubt that the resurrection happened, how will you go about investigating the facts more thoroughly?

If Jesus is your Lord, thank him for being not a dead ideal but a Person who lives, and allow him to be more and more involved in your life.

If you are unsure whether Jesus rose physically from the dead, commit yourself to investigating further.

For further reading: Chapters four and five of Basic Christianity.

Study Five
The Meaning of the Cross

1 Peter 2:21-25

*C*hristianity is a rescue religion. It declares that God has taken the initiative in Jesus Christ to deliver us from our sins. This is the main theme of the Bible.

> You are to give him the name Jesus, because he will save his people from their sins. (Matthew 1:21)

> The Son of Man came to seek and to save the lost. (Luke 19:10)

> Here is a trustworthy saying that deserves full acceptance: Christ Jesus came into the world to save sinners. (1 Timothy 1:15)

> We have seen and testify that the Father has sent his Son to be the Savior of the world. (1 John 4:14)

Through Jesus Christ the Savior, we can be brought out of exile and reconciled to God. We can be born again, receive a new nature and be set free from our moral bondage. And we can have the old discords replaced by a fellowship of love.

Open

In the nineteenth century a liberal optimism flourished. It was then widely believed that human nature was fundamentally good, that evil was largely caused by ignorance and bad housing, and that education and social reform would enable us to live together in happiness and goodwill. John F. Kennedy and Martin Luther King Jr. promoted this philosophy in more recent years.

☐ What evidence do you see today that such optimism about human nature was well founded?

☐ What evidence do you see that is was unrealistic?

☐ What evidence do you find in your own life that you need to be rescued—not from external problems but from undesirable characteristics within yourself?

Study

Read 1 Peter 2:21-25:

[21] To this you were called, because Christ suffered for you, leaving you an example, that you should follow in his steps.

[22] "He committed no sin, and no deceit was found in his mouth."
[23] When they hurled their insults at him, he did not retaliate; when he suffered, he made no threats. Instead, he entrusted himself to him who judges justly. [24] He himself bore our sins in his body on the tree, so that we might die to sins and live for righteousness; by his wounds you have been healed. [25] For you were like sheep going astray, but now you have returned to the Shepherd and Overseer of your souls.

Isaiah 53:5
9
12

1. What two purposes does Peter put forth for Jesus' death?

2. In verse 24 "the tree" refers to the cross. When Christ willingly died there, what did he accomplish for sinful humanity (v. 24)?

3. Why would Christ's death as an example be insufficient to gain God's forgiveness for our sins?

4. Do you think of Jesus' death as only an example, or do you believe that he also bore your sins? Explain your answer.

5. How does Jesus' behavior before his enemies show his confidence in the purpose of his death?

6. What response from believers in Jesus does Peter anticipate (vv. 24-25)?

7. How does Peter's anticipated response in verses 24-25 compare to your response to what Jesus did on the cross?

Commit ──────────────────────────────

☐ How have your loyalties been changed because Jesus died for you?

☐ What can you do to demonstrate your change in loyalties?

Offer your life to Christ and accept his willing sacrifice for your sins—whether today for the first time or renewing your commitment to him.

For further reading: Chapters six and seven of Basic Christianity.

Study Six
The Spirit of Christ

John 16:5-16

*C*an human nature be changed? Is it possible to make a sour person sweet, a proud person humble or a selfish person unselfish? The Bible declares emphatically that these miracles can take place. It is part of the glory of the gospel. Jesus Christ offers to change not only our standing before God but our very nature. He spoke to Nicodemus of the indispensable necessity of a new birth, and his words are still applicable to us: "Truly, truly, I say to you, unless one is born anew, he cannot see the kingdom of God. . . . Do not marvel that I said to you, 'You must be born anew' " (John 3:3-7 RSV).

Paul's statement is in some ways even more dramatic, for he blurts out, in a sentence which has no verbs: "If anyone in Christ—new creation!" (my translation of 2 Corinthians 5:17). Here then is the possibility of which the New Testament speaks—a new heart, a new nature, a new birth, a new creation.

This tremendous inward change is the work of the Holy Spirit.

Open

☐ How would you like to be different?

__I'd like to change my attitude toward life.

__I'd like to be less apprehensive about the future.

__I'd be more courageous.

__I'd be more loving toward people.

__I'd be more sincere.

__I like myself the way I am.

☐ What do you think keeps you from making those changes?

☐ What are some of the changes you believe the Holy Spirit has already made in your life?

Study

Read John 16:5-16 (Jesus said this to his disciples just before he was arrested and crucified):

[5]"Now I am going to him who sent me, yet none of you asks me, 'Where are you going?' [6]Because I have said these things, you are filled with grief. [7]But I tell you the truth: It is for your good that I am going away. Unless I go away, the Counselor will not come to you; but if I go, I will send him to you. [8]When he

comes, he will convict the world of guilt in regard to sin and righteousness and judgment: [9]in regard to sin, because men do not believe in me; [10]in regard to righteousness, because I am going to the Father, where you can see me no longer; [11]and in regard to judgment, because the prince of this world now stands condemned.

[12]"I have much more to say to you, more than you can now bear. [13]But when he, the Spirit of truth, comes, he will guide you into all truth. He will not speak on his own; he will speak only what he hears, and he will tell you what is yet to come. [14]He will bring glory to me by taking from what is mine and making it known to you. [15]All that belongs to the Father is mine. That is why I said the Spirit will take from what is mine and make it known to you.

[16]"In a little while you will see me no more, and then after a little while you will see me."

---

1. How did Jesus comfort his disciples in their alarm that he was leaving them?

---

2. What words indicate that the Counselor, or Spirit, is not a feeling or impersonal force, but a Person?

3. Jesus tells his disciples that this Counselor, the Spirit of truth, would do particular things for the "world" (nonbelievers). What were those things?

4. How would the Spirit help those who believe in Jesus?

5. What aspect of the Spirit's work gives him the name "Spirit of truth"?

6. Earlier Jesus said, "he [the Holy Spirit] lives with you and will be in you" (John 14:17). How does this promise make a new heart, a new nature, a new birth, a new creation possible in our everyday lives?

Commit

☐ How will you respond to Jesus' gift of the Holy Spirit to teach, guide and empower you in your Christian life?

☐ What changes do you think the Holy Spirit would like to make in you—with your cooperation?

Obey the prompting of the Spirit of Christ today. Give Christ permission to teach you and change you from the inside out, not only today but every day.

For further reading: Chapters eight and nine of Basic Christianity.

Responding to Christ

Are you a Christian? A real and committed Christian? Your answer depends on another question—not whether you go to church or not, believe certain creeds or doctrines or not, or lead a decent life or not (important as all these are in their place), but rather this: on which side of the door is Jesus Christ? Is he inside or outside? That is the crucial issue.

One verse in the Bible, which has helped many seekers (including myself) to understand the step of faith we have to take, contains the words of Christ himself. He says: "Here I am! I stand at the door and knock. If anyone hears my voice and opens the door, I will come in and eat with him, and he with me" (Revelation 3:20).

Perhaps you are ready to open the door to Christ. I suggest that you get away alone to pray. Confess your sins to God, and forsake them. Thank Jesus Christ that he died for your sake and in your place. Then open the door and ask him to come in as your personal Savior and Lord.

You might find it a help to echo this prayer in your heart:

Lord Jesus Christ, I acknowledge that I have gone my own way. I have sinned in thought, word and deed. I am sorry for my sins.

I turn from them in repentance.

I believe that you died for me, bearing my sins in your own body. I thank you for your great love.

Now I open the door. Come in, Lord Jesus. Come in as my Savior, and cleanse me. Come in as my Lord, and take control of me. And I will serve as you give me strength all my life. Amen.

If you have prayed this prayer and meant it, humbly thank Christ that he has come in. For he said he would. Now he calls us to follow him.

For further reading: Chapters ten and eleven of Basic Christianity.

Guidelines for Leaders

Leading a Bible discussion can be an enjoyable and rewarding experience. But it can also be intimidating—especially if you've never done it before. If this is how you feel, you're in good company.

Remember when God asked Moses to lead the Israelites out of Egypt? Moses replied, "O Lord, please send someone else to do it" (Exodus 4:13). But God gave Moses the help (human and divine) he needed to be a strong leader.

Leading a Bible discussion is not difficult if you follow certain guidelines. You don't need to be an expert on the Bible or a trained teacher. The suggestions listed below can help you to effectively fulfill your role as leader—and enjoy doing it.

Preparing for the Study

1. As you study the passage ahead of time, ask God to help you understand it and apply it in your own life. Unless this happens, you will not be prepared to lead others. Pray too for the various

members of the group. Ask God to open your hearts to the message of his Word and motivate you to action.

2. Read the introduction to the entire guide to get an overview of the subject at hand and the issues which will be explored.

3. Be ready for the "Open" questions with a personal story or example. The group will be only as vulnerable and open as its leader.

4. As you begin preparing for each study, read and reread the assigned Bible passage to familiarize yourself with it. You may want to look up the passage in a Bible so that you can see its context.

5. This study guide is based on the New International Version of the Bible. That is what is reproduced in your guide. It will help you and the group if you use this translation as the basis for your study and discussion.

6. Carefully work through each question in the study. Spend time in meditation and reflection as you consider how to respond.

7. Write your thoughts and responses in the space provided in the study guide. This will help you to express your understanding of the passage clearly.

8. It might help you to have a Bible dictionary handy. Use it to look up any unfamiliar words, names or places. (For additional help on how to study a passage, see chapter five of *Leading Bible Discussions*, IVP.)

9. Take the final (application) questions and the "Commit" portion of each study seriously. Consider what this means for your life, what changes you may need to make in your lifestyle and/or what actions you can take in your church or with people you know. Remember that the group will follow your lead in responding to the studies.

Leading the Study

1. Be sure everyone in your group has a study guide and Bible. Encourage the group to prepare beforehand for each discussion by reading the introduction to the guide and by working through the questions in the study.

2. At the beginning of your first time together, explain that these studies are meant to be discussions, not lectures. Encourage the members of the group to participate. However, do not put pressure on those who may be hesitant to speak during the first few sessions.

3. Begin the study on time. Open with prayer, asking God to help the group understand and apply the passage.

4. Have a group member read the introductory paragraph at the beginning of the discussion. This will remind the group of the topic of the study.

5. Every study begins with a section called *Open*. These "approach" questions are meant to be asked before the passage is read. They are important for several reasons.

First, there is always a stiffness that needs to be overcome before people will begin to talk openly. A good question will break the ice.

Second, most people will have lots of different things going on in their minds (dinner, an exam, an important meeting coming up, how to get the car fixed) that have nothing to do with the study. A creative question will get their attention and draw them into the discussion.

Third, approach questions can reveal where our thoughts or feelings need to be transformed by Scripture. That is why it is especially important not to read the passage before the approach question is asked. The passage will tend to color the honest reactions people would otherwise give, because they feel they are supposed to think the way the Bible does.

6. Have a group member read aloud the passage to be studied.

7. As you ask the questions, keep in mind that they are designed to be used just as they are written. You may simply read them aloud. Or you may prefer to express them in your own words.

There may be times when it is appropriate to deviate from the study guide. For example, a question may already have been answered. If so, move on to the next question. Or someone may raise an important question not covered in the guide. Take time to discuss it, but try to keep the group from going off on tangents.

8. Avoid answering your own questions. Repeat or rephrase them if necessary until they are clearly understood. An eager group quickly becomes passive and silent if members think the leader will give all the *right* answers.

9. Don't be afraid of silence. People may need time to think about the question before formulating their answers.

10. Don't be content with just one answer. Ask, "What do the rest of you think?" or, "Anything else?" until several people have given answers to a question.

11. Acknowledge all contributions. Be affirming whenever possible. Never reject an answer. If it is clearly off-base, ask, "Which verse led you to that conclusion?" or, "What do the rest of you think?"

12. Don't expect every answer to be addressed to you, even though this will probably happen at first. As group members become more at ease, they will begin to truly interact with each other. This is one sign of healthy discussion.

13. Don't be afraid of controversy. It can be stimulating! If you don't resolve an issue completely, don't be frustrated. Move on and keep it in mind for later. A subsequent study may solve the problem.

14. Periodically summarize what the group has said about the passage. This helps to draw together the various ideas mentioned and gives continuity to the study. But don't preach.

15. Don't skip over the application questions at the end of each study. It's important that we each apply the message of the passage to ourselves in a specific way. Be willing to get things started by describing how you have been affected by the study.

Depending on the makeup of your group and the length of time you've been together, you may or may not want to discuss the "Commit" section. If not, allow the group to read it and reflect on it silently. Encourage members to make specific commitments and to write them in their study guide. Ask them the following week how they did with their commitments.

16. Conclude your time together with conversational prayer. Ask for God's help in following through on the commitments you've made.

17. End on time.

Many more suggestions and helps are found in *The Big Book on Small Groups, Small Group Leaders' Handbook* and *Good Things Come in Small Groups* (IVP). Reading through one of these books would be worth your time.

Study Notes

General Note. This guide is intended to be for both Christians and non-Christians. Christians will benefit from a deeper knowledge of who Christ is. Seekers will have an opportunity to learn more about Christ and perhaps make a decision about whether they will follow him. Depending on the makeup of your group, you may want to direct the application to one audience or the other—or you may have both kinds of group members.

Study One. Are You Ready to Meet Christ? Mark 10:17-31.

Purpose: To respond to God's initiative toward us by seeking him with an open mind.

Question 2. Jesus "went to the heart of the man's problem, his devotion to his wealth rather than to God. Therein lay the one thing he lacked. In order to follow Jesus, he must remove the obstacle, his love of money. It was not works of charity that would gain for him eternal life; it was becoming identified with Christ" (Donald W. Burdick in *The Wycliffe Bible Commentary*, ed. Everett F. Harrison [Nashville: Southwestern Company, 1962], p. 1010).

Question 4. The Gospel of Luke reveals that the man was also a "ruler" (Luke 18:18), no doubt a ruler in the synagogue. Because he would have considered himself learned in the teachings of God, he may have felt the idea of giving up his wealth was an insult to his understanding of the Law. He may also have felt great fear at the possibility of having to choose between his wealth and eternal life.

Question 7. The Greek word translated "gospel," *euangelion*, "originally denoted a reward for good tidings; later, the idea of reward dropped, and the word stood for the good news itself. . . . In the New Testament it denotes the good tidings of the Kingdom of God and of salvation through Christ" (W. E. Vine, *An Expository Dictionary of New Testament Words* [London: Oliphants, 1940], 2:167). Some Christians give up close relationships and physical security for the sake of telling the good news of Jesus, and they testify to the fact that God provides alternate "home" and "family." Though persecutions will come too, everywhere God has a place and people for those who follow him.

Study Two. The Claims of Christ. John 8:51-59.
Purpose: To consider the implications of Jesus' claim to equality with God.
Question 2. "It was not physical life and physical death of which Jesus was thinking. He meant that, for the man who fully accepted him, there was no such thing as death. Death had lost its finality. . . . The man who accepts Jesus has entered into a relationship with God which neither time nor eternity can sever" (William Barclay, *The Gospel of John* [Philadelphia: Westminster Press, 2d ed., 1956], 2:38).
Question 3. "Jesus is the Lord incarnate, and thus he himself

bears this divine name. He is not simply a courier of revelation like Moses. He is revelation" (G. M. Burge, " 'I Am' Sayings," in *Dictionary of Jesus and the Gospels*, ed. Joel B. Green, Scot McKnight and I. Howard Marshall [Downers Grove, Ill.: Inter-Varsity Press, 1992], p. 356).

Study Three. The Character of Christ. John 13:1-17.
Purpose: To observe that there is no discrepancy between Jesus' words and his deeds.
Question 1. "It was just at that time when God was nearest to Him that Jesus went to the depths and the limits of His service of men. To wash the feet of the guests at a feast was the office of a slave. The disciples of the Rabbis were supposed to render their masters personal service, but a service like this would never have been dreamed of. The wonderful thing about Jesus was that His nearness to God, so far from separating Him from men, brought Him nearer than ever to men" (Barclay, *Gospel of John*, p. 160).
Question 2. In a parody of Jesus' knowledge, religious cult leaders typically assume absolute power, think God sent them, and believe they will die in some dramatic way. Often they lead their deluded followers to tragic fates. Jesus' act of serving his disciples by washing their feet is in absolute contrast to a cult leader's manipulative and egotistical behavior.
Question 4. Though he knelt before them doing the work of a slave, Jesus was not groveling before his disciples. His act of service came from his strong sense of who he was. He was confident of his role and his identity as the Son of God, and he stayed in command of the situation, as indicated in his words to Peter.
Question 5. For me there is no clearer or more compelling

evidence for the deity of Jesus than the extraordinary paradox between his lofty claims and his lowly conduct. Christ claimed to have come from God and to be the Lord and teacher of humanity. Yet here he is on his hands and knees washing their feet. Their Lord became their servant.

Study Four. The Resurrection of Christ. Luke 24:36-48.

Purpose: To examine some of the evidence that Jesus Christ conquered death and rose physically from the grave.

Questions 2-3. Jesus' hands and feet still bore the marks of crucifixion. A crucified person "was fastened to the cross by nails through the hands or wrists, and through the feet or above the heels" (Pierson Parker, "Crucifixion," in *Interpreter's Dictionary of the Bible*, ed. George A. Buttrick [Nashville: Abingdon, 1962], p. 747). One disciple, Thomas, was not there at this appearance and said he would not believe until he saw the nail marks as well as the wound in Jesus' side from a soldier's spear. Jesus returned and showed Thomas his wounds, even inviting Thomas to "reach out your hand and put it into my side" (John 20:24-27).

Question 4. Earlier that same day, during his walk with the two on the road to Emmaus, "beginning with Moses and all the Prophets, he explained to them what was said in all the Scriptures concerning himself." Clearly Jesus identified himself as the Messiah whom the Jewish Scriptures prophesied.

Question 5. In the New Testament we have the record of those who saw him, and there is much evidence for the historical accuracy and reliability of those records. There are other non-Christian historical documents and the writings of the early church leaders. And there is the testimony of all Christians through the ages who have experienced his life-changing power.

Study Five. The Meaning of the Cross. 1 Peter 2:21-25.
Purpose: To consider how Christ's death on the cross can affect the quality of our lives today.
Question 1. Earlier Peter quoted Isaiah 53:9 as a prophecy of Jesus' sinlessness. Now he refers to Isaiah 53:12—"For he bore the sin of many"—and 53:5—"by his wounds we are healed." Our sins deserve God's punishment, but Jesus died willingly as our substitute.
Question 3. Jesus did not try to escape or resist his enemies; he did not die as their helpless victim. He knew who he was, why he was there and why these terrible events must happen; he was sure that salvation for others was possible only through his death.
Question 4. Not only would much in the Gospels remain mysterious if Christ's death were purely an example, but our human need would remain unsatisfied. We need more than an example; we need a Savior. An example can stir our imagination, kindle our idealism and strengthen our resolve, but it cannot cleanse the defilement of our past sins, bring peace to our troubled conscience or reconcile us to God.

Study Six. The Spirit of Christ. John 16:5-16.
Purpose: To respond to the Holy Spirit as he seeks to work changes in us.
Question 2. Jesus refers to the Holy Spirit not as "it" but by the personal pronoun "he." The Spirit deals with people, hears, communicates, guides, teaches. A warm feeling or a jolt of energy can't do those things; those are the activities of a person.
Question 4. It is no good giving me a play like *Hamlet* or *King*

Lear, and telling me to write a play like that. Shakespeare could do it; I can't. And it is no good showing me a life like the life of Jesus and telling me to live a life like that. Jesus could do it; I can't. But if the Spirit of Jesus could come and live in me, then I could live a life like that.

Question 6. The apostle Paul wrote: "So I say, live by the Spirit, and you will not gratify the desires of the sinful nature" (Galatians 5:16). After describing the acts of the sinful nature, he continued, "But the fruit of the Spirit is love, joy, peace, patience, kindness, goodness, faithfulness, gentleness and self-control" (5:22).

Christian Basics Bible Studies from InterVarsity Press

Christian Basics are the keys to becoming a mature disciple. The studies in these guides, based on material from some well-loved books, will take you through key Scripture passages and help you to apply biblical truths to your life. Each guide has six studies for individuals or groups.

Character: Who You Are When No One's Looking by Bill Hybels. We all do our best when others are watching. But what about when no one is looking? That's where character comes in, giving us consistency when it's just between God and us.

Courage. Discipline. Vision. Endurance. Compassion. Self-sacrifice. The qualities covered in this Bible study guide provide a foundation for character. With this foundation and God's guidance, we can maintain character even when we face temptations and troubles.

Christ: Basic Christianity by John Stott. God himself is seeking us. Through his Son, Jesus Christ, God wants to offer us his love.

But who is this Jesus Christ? These studies explore the person and character of this man who has altered the face of history.

Come, and discover him for the first time or in a new and deeper way.

Commitment: My Heart—Christ's Home by Robert Boyd Munger. What would it be like to have Christ come into the home of our hearts? Moving from room to room with him, we discover what he desires for us. Are we prepared to meet with him daily in our living room? in our recreation room? in the study? What about that dark closet that needs cleaning out?

These studies will take you through six of the rooms of your heart, helping you to see aspects of your Christian life as Jesus sees them. You will be stretched and enriched by your personal meetings with Christ in each study.

Prayer: Too Busy Not to Pray by Bill Hybels. Most of us have trouble finding time to pray. There's so much going on—work, church, school, family, relationships: the list is never-ending. Someone always seems to need something from us. But time for God, time to pray, seems impossible to find.

These studies are designed to help you slow down and listen to God. But they don't stop there! They also help you to learn how to respond. As a result, you will grow closer to God and experience the benefits of spending time with him.

Priorities: Tyranny of the Urgent by Charles Hummel. Have you ever wished for a thirty-hour day? Every week we leave a trail of unfinished tasks. Unanswered letters, unvisited friends and unread books haunt our waking moments. We desperately need relief.

These studies are designed to help you put your life back in order by discovering what is *really* important. Find out what God's priorities are for you.

Scripture: God's Word for Contemporary Christians by John Stott. What is the place of Scripture in our lives? We know it is important—God's Word to us—but how can it make a difference to us each day?

In this guide, John Stott will show you the power Scripture can have in your life. These studies will help you make the Bible your anchor to God in the face of the temptation and corruption that are all around.

Work: Serving God by What We Do by Ben Patterson. "I can serve God in church, but can I serve him on the job?" In the factory, in the office, in the home, on the road, on the farm—Ben Patterson says we can give glory to God wherever he calls us.

Work, even what seems to us the most mundane, is what God created us for. He is our employer. These studies will show you how your work can become meaningful and satisfying.

Worship: Serving God with Our Praise by Ben Patterson. Our deepest need can be filled only as we come to our Creator in worship. This is the divine drama in which we are all invited to participate, not as observers but as performers. True worship will transform every part of our lives, and these studies will help you to understand and experience the glory of praising God.